NEW ENGLAND AQUARIUM

OFFICIAL COMMEMORATIVE GUIDE

BECKON BOOKS

BREAKTHROUGH

In 1980, Aquarium scientists discovered a small group of North Atlantic right whales in the Bay of Fundy between Maine and Nova Scotia. Until then, the scientific community had believed that right whales  were nearly extinct. It turned out that the right whales were calving off the coasts of Georgia and northeastern Florida and migrating to the Bay of Fundy. The Aquarium has been working to save the remaining North Atlantic right whales ever since.

THE FIRST MODERN AQUARIUM

In the late 1950s, New England businessman David B. Stone stood on a crumbling pier at Boston's dilapidated Central Wharf and had a revolutionary idea. What if the decrepit parking lot surrounding him were transformed into a modern attraction—a source of local pride and beauty that featured a place where Boston's residents and visiting tourists could connect with the harbor, ocean and marine life?

A dozen years later, thanks to the efforts of Stone and several other founders, this vision became a reality. When the New England Aquarium opened on June 20, 1969, it ushered in a whole new era of modern aquariums. Its exhibits were a departure from the small recessed tanks—presented like portraits in a museum—that characterized most other aquariums until that time. Out front, visitors were welcomed by Atlantic harbor seals displayed in an open-air exhibit. Inside, guests could get nose-to-nose with a rich variety of marine life housed in the Giant Ocean Tank, a four-story, 200,000-gallon saltwater tank.

The quality of the Aquarium's immersion experience was unprecedented, and it has inspired virtually every modern aquarium built since. Today, in addition to exhibiting both rare and endangered marine life, the New England Aquarium works on solutions to some of the most challenging problems facing the oceans, making it a global leader in ocean exploration, marine conservation and education.

ON CENTRAL WHARF
The New England Aquarium is one of Boston's most popular attractions and a major resource for public education.

SEA TURTLE RESCUE
Over the past 15 years, the Aquarium has rehabilitated and released hundreds of endangered sea turtles, such as this one at top.

AQUARIUM BEGINNINGS
Due to its massive size, the Giant Ocean Tank (pictured in the background) was built first; the rest of the Aquarium was constructed around it.

FINS ON FILM
The Matthew and Marcia Simons IMAX® Theatre shows animals that are too large, too dangerous or too endangered to exhibit at the Aquarium.

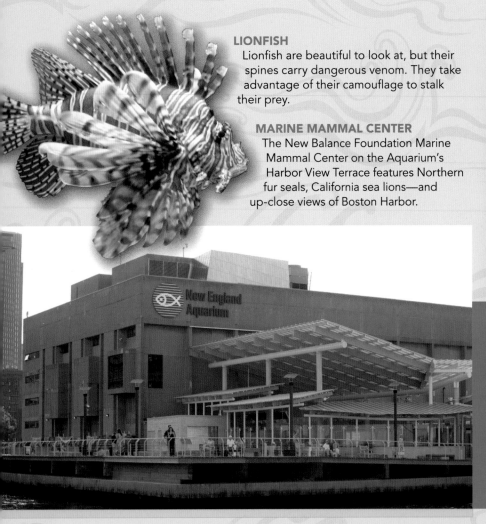

LIONFISH
Lionfish are beautiful to look at, but their spines carry dangerous venom. They take advantage of their camouflage to stalk their prey.

MARINE MAMMAL CENTER
The New Balance Foundation Marine Mammal Center on the Aquarium's Harbor View Terrace features Northern fur seals, California sea lions—and up-close views of Boston Harbor.

NEW ENGLAND AQUARIUM WHALE WATCH

The coastline off Boston and Cape Cod has been cited as one the top ten whale watching destinations on the planet—and voters on Boston.com's A-List named the New England Aquarium Whale Watch the area's best experience. Guests are whisked 45 minutes east to the Stellwagen Bank National Marine

Sanctuary at the mouth of the Massachusetts Bay. The sanctuary is a rich feeding ground for humpback, minke and finback whales as well as the critically endangered North Atlantic right whales. It also hosts Atlantic white-sided dolphins, pilot whales, harbor porpoises and seals, sea birds and turtles. Trained naturalists are onboard every trip to discuss the behaviors, conservation status and migratory patterns of the 17 species of marine mammals that frequent the sanctuary's fertile underwater plateau. Best of all, whale sightings are guaranteed! In the rare event no whales are spotted, passengers receive a complimentary New England Aquarium Whale Watch ticket for use later in the season.

A WATERFRONT REVIVAL
When David B. Stone and others decided to build a new public aquarium, Central Wharf was run-down and neglected. This late-1960s photograph shows the Aquarium, in the foreground, near completion.

SPECIAL DELIVERY
Food for many of the inhabitants in the Giant Ocean Tank is readied in a stainless steel–clad food prep room. Sea turtles and sharks are regularly fed food such as vitamin-packed squid.

ANIMAL CARE AND NUTRITION

With more than 26,000 fishes, mammals, birds, reptiles, amphibians and invertebrates onsite, every day is an adventure for the Aquarium's husbandry staff (aquarists and trainers) and the "Wet Vets" in the Aquarium's Animal Health Department. They make rounds each morning to view the animals and go over any existing cases or medical issues that might have cropped up overnight—from a tiny cardinal fish with a buoyancy problem to a 5-foot-long green moray eel with a waning appetite. Sick animals might need to be removed so the vets can examine them in the Aquarium's state-of-the-art medical facility. There, the doctors perform everything from radiographs (X-rays) to complex surgeries.

Of course, health is closely related with nutrition. Each day, the Aquarium's husbandry staff prepares an average of 200 pounds of species-appropriate food in stainless steel–clad food prep rooms. The animals in the largest exhibit, the Giant Ocean Tank, are fed four times a day. Over in the Marine Mammal Center, the seals consume another 80 pounds of herring, capelin and squid daily. The sand tiger and nurse sharks are fed large fish and squid regularly to ensure they won't snack on their fellow inhabitants.

The Aquarium uses different methods to feed each species. Some of the sharks are fed on a stick to protect staff from powerful jaws, and the penguins are fed by hand to make sure each bird gets the proper amount of nutrition and supplements. In contrast, the shorebirds forage for their food, which is left out in bowls or buried in the wet sand, where the birds can find their next meal just like they would in the wild.

GENTLE DENTAL WORK
To prevent plaque and gingivitis, the trainers in the Marine Mammal Center brush the seals' teeth. They use a special malt-flavored tooth-paste and a rinse that is applied directly to the seals' gums.

ROUTINE EXAMS
Each of the more than 90 penguins at the Aquarium gets an annual check-up. This endangered African penguin pictured at top is getting weighed. Individuals of this species can weigh up to nine pounds and reach 25 inches in height.

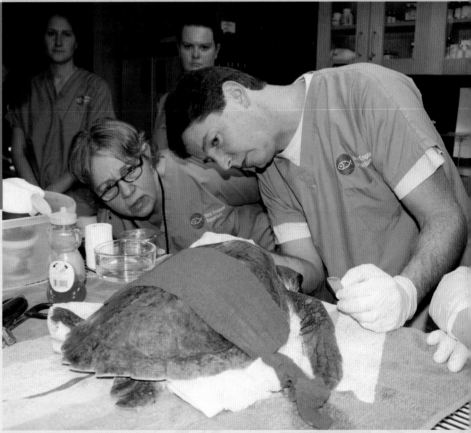

A MARINE HOSPITAL
Rescued sea turtles are brought to the Animal Rescue Team and veterinarians at the Aquarium. Many suffer from extreme hypothermia, dehydration, pneumonia and shell or bone fractures.

PENGUINS

With more than 90 birds swimming and diving through 150,000 gallons of clean, filtered salt water from Boston Harbor, the penguin exhibit is one of the Aquarium's most popular attractions. Located on the first floor, the exhibit surrounds the Giant Ocean Tank and can be seen from almost everywhere in the facility. Visitors can watch aquarists and volunteers hand-feed the penguins twice a day or see a Penguin Presentation to learn the species' characteristics and the conservation issues they face. Three species typically call the Aquarium home: African penguins, also known as jackass penguins due to their loud donkey bray; southern rockhopper penguins, which have wild yellow feathers on their heads; and little blue penguins, the smallest penguin species in the world.

The New England Aquarium is committed to penguin conservation. Since 1969, it has successfully hatched and raised more than 95 African, rockhopper and little blue penguin chicks. In the wild, penguins face many natural threats. Sharks and fur seals hunt them in the water, and predatory birds, along with introduced species such as mongooses and cats, prey on them on land. Southern rockhopper penguins are threatened, and their northern cousins (which have been on exhibit at the Aquarium) are endangered. African penguins are also endangered due to climate change, pollution, introduced predators and overfishing. At the beginning of the 20th century, there were no more than 575,000 adult African penguins; today, an estimated 52,000 remain.

A SHORE THING
Penguins come onshore to breed, molt and raise chicks. African penguins and little blue penguins nest in burrows on or near scrubby temperate beaches, while rockhoppers prefer rocky subantarctic islands.

LITTLE BLUE PENGUIN
Found exclusively in Australia and New Zealand, little blue penguins like the one seen at top are the smallest of all 18 penguin species. They weigh one to three pounds.

AFRICAN PENGUIN
African penguins are native to coastal waters and islands of Namibia and South Africa. In the wild, their lifespan is 10 to 15 years. African penguins at the Aquarium have lived to be 35.

ROCKHOPPER PENGUIN
Rockhopper penguins hop with extraordinary agility to get around the steep, rocky islands where they live and breed.

DID YOU KNOW?

Rockhopper penguins return to the same breeding site each year and even use the same nest when possible. They are known to breed in colonies of up to 100,000 birds.

PENGUINS

DIVE BOMBER

Penguins can dive deeper and swim faster than any other bird. As powerful predators, some species can reach bursts of speed of 20 miles per hour. Some species spend up to 75 percent of their lives at sea.

HABITAT HOUSEKEEPING

Aquarists and volunteers clean the rock islands in the penguin exhibit every day. The exhibit also has sprinklers on each island that activate periodically throughout the day to wash guano (penguin poop) off the islands and keep things clean.

BOND, BREED AND BURROW

In the wild, African penguins breed in huge, noisy colonies. They usually lay two eggs in burrows—bowl-shaped depressions underground that protect the eggs from the sun and predators. African penguins form tight pair bonds, and both parents incubate the eggs and feed the chicks for two to four months.

AN INTERACTIVE EXHIBIT

Visitors can watch the penguins being fed twice a day. The penguin exhibit also has several interactive features, such as an underwater periscope and a panel of penguin sounds.

RIGHT OR LEFT WING?

Each penguin is identified by a bracelet on its wing. Males have bracelets on the left, females on the right.

SMALL STEPS FORWARD

Despite recent decreases in population, little blue penguins continue to live in large numbers and maintain an expansive habitat. Measures are in place to protect them from introduced predators, such as dogs, cats and foxes.

GLOBAL EXPLORERS

In the fall of 2011, the Aquarium sent penguin aquarist Paul Leonard to Dassen Island in South Africa to study African penguins. Egg harvesting on Dassen was rampant during

the first half of the 20th century, with up to 600,000 eggs being collected each year. In the 1960s, the penguin population began to diminish, and the practice was outlawed. Today, as few as 8,000 African penguins remain there. By conducting nest surveys, studying breeding conditions and attaching GPS data loggers to penguins on Dassen, researchers hope to determine why the population is still declining and take steps to bolster it.

NEW ARRIVALS
These African penguin chicks hatched at
the Aquarium. As they would in the wild,
African penguin parents incubate the eggs
and feed the chicks for two to four months.

LIFT OFF
Penguins, such as these rockhoppers, lift their wings to cool off. Exposing the underside of their wings releases heat and cools their blood.

SOMETHING FISHY
The penguins are fed by hand to make sure that each gets the proper amount of nutrition, which includes calories and supplements.

RESCUING PENGUINS IN SOUTH AFRICA

On June 23, 2000, the damaged bulk ore carrier *MV Treasure* sank, spilling 1,300 tons of bunker oil off the coast of South Africa. The spill occurred between Robben and Dassen Islands, two of the largest breeding islands for African penguins, in the middle of an otherwise successful breeding season. Within days, thousands of oiled penguins started showing up on the beaches along South Africa and its islands.

For penguins, oil spills are disastrous. When oil gets in water, it sits on the surface, and as penguins come up to breathe, they are covered in it. Oil ruins the waterproofing qualities of their feathers. If penguins remain in the cold ocean water, they can become hypothermic, but if they stay on land, they can starve.

The Aquarium sent exhibit manager Heather Urquhart to South Africa to assist with the *Treasure* spill and help keep the 20,000 oiled penguins alive, hand-feeding them while they waited to be de-oiled. When it was time to clean them, all of the penguins were hand-washed with dishwashing soap and rinsed thoroughly to remove all the oil. After shampooing, they were rinsed in warm water and then put into cages with air dryers. The penguins stayed in the rescue facility until they were healthy enough to be released into the wild. Experts estimate more than 90 percent of them were saved.

SHARK AND RAY TOUCH TANK

The Trust Family Foundation Shark and Ray Touch Tank features more than 140 individual sharks and rays in a 25,000-gallon mangrove-themed tank. Shallow edges and viewing windows along one side of the exhibit allow visitors to reach out and gently touch 16 different species of sharks and rays, including cownose rays, bonnethead sharks, Atlantic rays and epaulette sharks. The deep end of the exhibit gives the sharks and rays a place to rest.

The touch tank emphasizes the value of conserving essential coastal habitats, such as mangroves and lagoons, and the critical role of sharks and rays in maintaining a healthy ocean ecosystem. By providing a snapshot of their broad diversity, the touch tank also gives visitors a new perspective on sharks and rays. There are now more than 500 identified species of sharks, but only a few are considered dangerous to humans. In fact, humans are more likely to be killed by dogs, snakes and even mountain lions than by sharks. Unfortunately, humans reportedly kill 70 to 100 million sharks each year. As a result, it is estimated that roughly 20 percent of shark and ray species are on the brink of extinction— prompting many aquariums and conservation organizations to help create and promote solutions to the rapid disappearance of these vital ocean creatures.

A VITAL HABITAT
The shark and ray touch tank exhibit is based on a mangrove habitat. Many species rely on mangrove forests, including Kemp's ridley sea turtles, various sharks and an estimated 80 percent of the commercial fish in South Florida.

COWNOSE RAY
Cownose rays, like this one pictured at top, kick up underwater sandstorms when searching for food such as oysters, clams, snails and crabs.

A WIDE RANGE
Cownose rays can be up to 48 inches wide. They range from New England to the South Caribbean, including the Yucatan, northern parts of South America, western Africa and the Cape Verde Islands.

SWIM SCHOOL

Visitors reach out and touch some passing cownose rays. In the wild, these rays travel in large groups, or schools. They have been seen swimming between Florida and Mexico in schools of up to 10,000!

BONNETHEAD SHARK
The smallest species in the family of hammerhead-like sharks, bonnethead sharks can be up to five feet long. They live in subtropical regions in the Western Atlantic and Eastern Pacific Oceans.

GLOBAL EXPLORERS

Aquarium explorers study ecosystems around the world, and wherever they go they keep an eye out for sharks. Brian Skerry, a *National Geographic* photographer and Aquarium Explorer in Residence, has studied and observed scores of sharks from Mexico to the Phoenix Islands. He has photographed sharks serving different roles in reef communities, eating different foods, moving greater distances and generally "holding the fort." Sharks are a good indicator of an ecosystem's health. If there are many sharks, the ecosystem is producing lots of fishes for the sharks to eat. Ecosystems without many sharks usually don't have enough food or have problems with overfishing.

EPAULETTE SHARK AND WHITE SPOTTED BAMBOO SHARK
Epaulette sharks (left) eat bottom-dwelling invertebrates and small fish. White spotted bamboo sharks (right) are often found at the bottom of sandy mangrove habitats, where they are protected from larger predators.

RAY AND PREY
Although cownose rays can grow large enough to fend off most predators, they are still hunted by large sharks, such as great hammerhead and bull sharks.

DID YOU KNOW?

One shark can produce thousands of teeth in its lifetime. Sharks have skeletons made out of cartilage, not bone, and their teeth are loosely embedded in their gums. When their teeth fall out, they are replaced with others from the row behind them. Depending on the species, sharks can have three to 15 rows of teeth.

BONNETHEAD SHARK
Despite pressures from both targeted and accidental fishing, bonnethead sharks remain abundant. At the last assessment, the species had some of the highest population growth rates calculated for sharks.

ATLANTIC HARBOR SEALS

The 46,000–gallon Atlantic harbor seal exhibit is located on the Front Plaza to the left of the Aquarium's front doors. Open to the New England weather—a typical habitat for western Atlantic harbor seals—it is the only exhibit that visitors can actually see before buying a ticket. Here, the Aquarium's seals play in deep, cool water and then haul out on the rocky outcrops for a snooze or a sunbath. The exhibit has training and enrichment sessions as well as seasonal interactive programs in which guests can go behind the scenes to feed and touch the harbor seals.

Harbor seals are generally found along the west coast of the Atlantic, from the coasts of Canada and Greenland to New Jersey. There are also populations of harbor seals in the temperate waters along the east coast of the Atlantic and the east coast of the Pacific. They can weigh up to 300 pounds and reach 5½ feet long. Their lifespan is approximately 25 years. Two families of harbor seals live at the Aquarium. Each seal looks different, with gray or brown hair and varied spots, and each has a distinct personality.

MEET AND GREET
The Aquarium offers special programs that allow visitors to go behind the scenes in the Atlantic harbor seal exhibit.

HAULING OUT
Harbor seals frequently rest on rocks out of the water, top. This behavior is called "hauling out."

FAMILY LIFE
Harbor seals do not form pair bonds. One male will breed with many females. After an 11-month pregnancy, females give birth to a single pup. The females rest and raise their pups on rocky beaches.

ATLANTIC HARBOR SEAL
In the wild, adult harbor seals are hunted by orcas, large sharks and polar bears. Smaller sharks, foxes and birds of prey will hunt pups.

DID YOU KNOW?

Harbor seals lose their coat of hair every summer. While they are molting, their appetite decreases, and they often aren't their usual spunky selves. Growing hair is hard work!

A SEAL MEAL
Seals at the Aquarium consume around 80 pounds of squid, capelin and herring daily.

ON THE PLAZA
The Atlantic harbor seal exhibit, located outside the building, is one of the first things visitors see when arriving at the Aquarium Plaza.

A DANCING DUO
Harbor seal training sessions often include behaviors such as blowing bubbles, waving to visitors and dancing.

HOOVER, THE TALKING SEAL

For many years, the New England Aquarium had its own talking seal. Hoover, an Atlantic harbor seal, was as well known in Boston as Ted Kennedy, and he spoke with a similar accent! Hoover's famous phrases included, "Hello there," "How are ya?" "Get outta here!" "Get over here," and "Hoover," which were accompanied by his signature guttural laugh. Hoover was the first non-human mammal to mimic human words.

Hoover was rescued as a baby in 1971. Realizing that he was an orphan, George and Alice Swallow brought him to their home in Maine, put him in a bathtub and fed him ground mackerel. He soon began to inhale his food, earning him the name "Hoover." Hoover quickly outgrew the bathtub and was moved to a pond behind the house, where he began to imitate the way people talked. When the Swallows brought Hoover to the Aquarium, he was four months old. George Swallow told Aquarium staff he thought the seal could talk, but no one at the Aquarium believed him. After a few years, however, Hoover's phrases became clearer, and scientists started researching his vocalizing abilities. The origin of his heavy Maine accent was a mystery until the researchers met the Swallows: Hoover talked just like them!

Hoover was featured on television and in many newspapers and magazines. He died of old age in 1985 and left several offspring. Some of his descendants still live at the Aquarium, including his grandson, Chacoda, who is mimicking phrases such as "How are you?" and "Hey."

Hoover received his own obituary in the *Boston Globe*.

PACIFIC REEF COMMUNITY

The Aquarium's serene Pacific Reef community recreates the tropical waters of a Pacific coral reef and highlights the rainbow-colored fishes that call it home. Designed and built by Aquarium artists, aquarists and researchers, the reef is home to more than 100 different kinds of tropical reef fishes. Here, coral cat sharks, epaulette sharks, unicorn tangs, bird wrasses, blue-striped cleaner wrasses and even a palette surgeonfish—which many guests recognize as Dory from *Finding Nemo*—hide among the corals and dart through the exhibit.

Coral reefs, and in particular Pacific reefs, are among the most diverse and oldest habitats in the world. Coral reefs protect shores from storm damage, provide food and are important sources of new medicines being developed to treat human disease. Unfortunately, most coral reefs are in decline due to overfishing, pollution and global warming. This affects not only the corals but also the thousands of species that depend on them.

DID YOU KNOW?

Since it was founded in 1999, the Marine Conservation Action Fund (MCAF) at the Aquarium has funded 100 projects and disbursed over $584,000 to protect highly vulnerable species and habitats.

BLUE-GREEN CHROMIS
A blue-green chromis swims beside a coral outcropping. This small species of damselfish lives in big schools, sheltered among corals or mangroves.

LAGOON TRIGGERFISH
Lagoon triggerfish, top, are sometimes called Picassofish because of their distinctive markings. They can reach up to 12 inches long.

MANDARINFISH
Mandarinfish have impressive colors that hold a deeper meaning for predators. These fish secrete toxic mucus. Their bright patterns warn predators to stay away.

YELLOW TANG
Yellow tang are a popular aquarium fish and a top marine fish export from Hawaii. While they are most often found in the Pacific Ocean, this species has also been seen off the coast of Florida.

BANNERFISH
Bannerfish are native to the Indo-Pacific. With their black and white stripes and yellow fins, these fish resemble moorish idols and are also known as pennant coralfish.

GLOBAL EXPLORERS

Over the years, Dr. Randi Rotjan, one of the Aquarium's associate scientists, has been on expeditions to Belize, Saudi Arabia, Panama, Indonesia and Kiribati (the Phoenix Islands) to conduct research on coral reefs and the effectiveness of marine protected areas. This is part of a long history of Aquarium coral reef habitat projects that include researchers Dr. Les Kaufman, Dr. Greg Stone and Dr. David Obura, and Fishes Department staffers Steve Bailey, Dan Laughlin, Brian Nelson and Peter Gawne. In collaboration with other institutions, the Aquarium team monitors the health of reefs in hopes of conserving their biodiversity around the world.

CORAL COLONIES
The Aquarium's living coral exhibits feature a variety of coral species, as shown below right. Corals are actually colonies of small animals; they require a carefully maintained habitat to survive.

CLOWNFISH
Clownfish have a symbiotic relationship with anemones. The stinging anemone keeps larger predators away from the clownfish, and the clownfish guards the anemone from smaller predators and helps clean between the anemone's tentacles.

SEMICIRCLE ANGELFISH
Semicircle angelfish will dramatically change color through their lifetime. Their sharp dorsal fins can be used for defense.

PHOENIX ISLANDS

The Phoenix Islands are located more than 1,000 miles southwest of Hawaii in the nation of Kiribati. This isolated island chain is home to one of Earth's last uninhabited and relatively intact oceanic coral archipelago ecosystems. There, the coral reefs teem with life, and the tropical sky is alive with seabirds. The Aquarium made its first visit to the Phoenix Islands in 2000 when staff members began working to preserve this irreplaceable ecosystem, performing hands-on scientific expeditions to explore and document the Phoenix Islands' incredible abundance, and conducting policy work to help preserve the region. Since that first visit, the New England Aquarium, in partnership with Kiribati, has led the charge to protect these islands and their reefs. In 2008, the Phoenix Islands Protected Area (PIPA)—a marine protected area about the size of the state of California—was established. In August 2010, PIPA was inscribed as a World Heritage site, the largest and deepest on Earth.

GIANT OCEAN TANK

The Giant Ocean Tank—a towering, four-story coral reef exhibit—is located in the middle of the Aquarium. The tank may be viewed from all sides, including the top level, where guests can look down into the water, participate in a "GOT Talk" or watch aquarist divers feed the animals. Measuring 23 feet deep by 40 feet wide, the tank holds 200,000 gallons of salt water that is filtered every 90 minutes. The water temperature is maintained between 74 degrees and 78 degrees Fahrenheit, mimicking seasonal fluctuations in the Bahamas.

The unchallenged star of the Giant Ocean Tank is Myrtle the green sea turtle, who has lived at the Aquarium since June 1970. Myrtle weighed 560 pounds at a recent checkup. Lifting a sea turtle of that size on a scale would be unsafe, so she was slung from a hanging scale in a cradle designed for underwater maneuvering. Myrtle shares the tank with more than 600 animals, including Kemp's ridley and loggerhead sea turtles, sand tiger sharks, barracuda, stingrays, moray eels and hundreds of colorful reef fishes.

GIANT OCEAN TANK
The Giant Ocean Tank is an accurate recreation of a Caribbean coral reef. The reef was designed by the Aquarium's husbandry, research and design staffers and was built and installed by the Aquarium's habitat fabrication team.

FISH ON STICKS
Some of the sharks in the Giant Ocean Tank are fed by stick to distance staff from their powerful jaws. In the wild, sand tiger sharks like this one use their sharp teeth to catch similar fishes, squid, crabs and lobsters.

SAND TIGER SHARK
Like many other shark species, sand tiger sharks like the one shown at top are classified as vulnerable to extinction. Millions of sharks are reportedly killed every year for their fins, cartilage, teeth and jaws.

LOGGERHEAD SEA TURTLE
Out of the seven species of sea turtles, three are present in the Giant Ocean Tank: loggerhead (shown here), green and Kemp's ridley sea turtles.

DID YOU KNOW?

Unlike human fingernails, turtle shells have nerve endings. Not only can turtles feel their shell being scratched . . . some of them like it. Myrtle, the Aquarium's resident green sea turtle, will follow divers around the Giant Ocean Tank until they scratch her back with a seashell.

IN A DAY'S WORK
A diver feeds a southern stingray in the Giant Ocean Tank. Aquarists and some experienced volunteers dive five times a day in the tank to feed the animals, observe animal behavior, maintain the habitat and conduct research activities, such as collecting larval fish.

GREEN SEA TURTLE

Myrtle, the green sea turtle, is the queen of the Giant Ocean Tank. Found in tropical to temperate waters worldwide, green sea turtles can reach up to five feet long and live 100 years or more.

BY THE NUMBERS

Every year, aquarists and volunteer divers conduct a census of the animals in the exhibit.

A LOCAL RESCUE

The Aquarium educates people to choose their pet marine animals wisely, since some can grow to an unmanageable size. When this happens, owners are put in a quandary: For various reasons, most aquariums cannot accept domestic animal donations. But domesticated animals should never be released back into the wild. They are unlikely to survive and could introduce diseases or other microorganisms to local populations.

At the New England Aquarium, however, one former pet was an exception: one of the green moray eels in the Giant Ocean Tank. In 2009, the Aquarium received a call from an owner in Billerica, Massachusetts, whose eel had outgrown his tank. Since there are very few home aquariums that can hold an adult moray eel of this species, the eel qualified as a rescue. Staff members brought him back to the Aquarium, transferred him to a large secure moray holding barrel, which is similar to a moray's cave in the wild, and placed him in a holding system behind the scenes for quarantine. After thirty days, he was ready to go on exhibit. The eel was introduced to his new habitat in the Giant Ocean Tank for three days while he stayed in his barrel, giving him time to acclimate. Once the lid was removed, he cautiously explored the exhibit, and within a few hours, he found a comfortable spot at the top of the reef.

IN THE TANK

A sand tiger shark approaches as an Aquarium diver works in the exhibit. They may look threatening, but sand tiger sharks are not dangerous to humans unless mishandled or provoked.

NASSAU GROUPER

The Nassau grouper, seen among the coral in the Giant Ocean Tank, makes a territorial thumping noise that warns other fishes to stay away.

CLIMATE CHANGE AND THE OCEANS

The New England Aquarium leads a nationwide collaborative of aquariums working together to educate millions of visitors about the impact of climate change on the oceans. The oceans have a central role in maintaining our climate. They absorb, store and then slowly release large quantities of heat, buffering the climate of the nearby land and, over time, the entire planet.

Climate change is largely due to increased amounts of greenhouse gases (e.g., carbon dioxide) in the atmosphere, which trap heat. Climate change has already caused an increase in sea surface temperatures. It is also causing sea levels to rise, both because water expands as it warms (thermal expansion) and because freshwater runoff into the oceans increases as mountain glaciers melt. In addition, scientists predict that climate change will cause the ice sheets that lie on top of Greenland and Antarctica to melt, further increasing the volume of water in the oceans. The oceans are Earth's largest carbon reservoir, holding many times as much carbon dioxide as the atmosphere. However, one consequence of increased carbon absorption in the oceans is that they are becoming more acidic, which reduces the ability of some marine calcifiers (shellfish, corals, diatoms) to form shells and skeletons.

Climate change creates other problems, too, such as increasing water temperatures above the tolerance limits of many animals (like corals) and melting floating sea ice, which threatens the animals that rely on it to hunt and reproduce (like polar bears and penguins). Rising sea levels will also have significant consequences for islands and low-lying coastal areas where millions of human beings reside, such as the cities of Boston and New York.

QUEEN TRIGGERFISH
This species preys on sea urchins by blowing them over and attacking them where their spines are short.

PROTECTING THE WATERS
An aquarist stands at the top of the Giant Ocean Tank's towering coral reef. By supporting important research on climate change, the Aquarium is working to protect the planet's largest and most valuable natural resource— the oceans.

SOUTHERN STINGRAY
In the wild, southern stingrays camouflage themselves by flipping sand onto themselves while on the ocean floor.

BREAKTHROUGH

In 2009, Aquarium scientist and Roger Williams University assistant professor Andrew L. Rhyne and Aquarium director of research Michael Tlusty teamed up with assistant curator of fishes Dan Laughlin and aquarist Chris Bauernfiend to hatch queen triggerfish from eggs collected in the Giant Ocean Tank. It was the first time this species was reared out of the wild.

PACIFIC NORTHWEST

Three exhibits on the third level feature animals native to the colder northern waters of the Pacific Coast. The largest species in the Pacific Northwest exhibits is the giant Pacific octopus. Native to the northern Pacific Ocean, these invertebrates are intelligent, have excellent eyesight and are very strong. They can grow to be 20 feet from tip to tip of their outstretched arms and weigh up to 150 pounds.

Elsewhere in these exhibits, visitors get a close-up look at other invertebrates, such as anemones and sea cucumbers. The exhibits also feature bat stars, which get their name from the joined area between their arms. This area looks like the webbing between the bones of a bat's wing. This adaptation may help the bat star withstand the force of crashing waves.

DID YOU KNOW?

Adult female giant Pacific octopuses lay up to 75,000 eggs. The females nurture their eggs until they are ready to hatch, which can take six months.

GIANT GREEN SEA ANEMONE
The Pacific tidal exhibit, which replicates tidal motion in the rocky Pacific Northwest, includes species such as this giant green sea anemone.

CLOSED ANEMONE
This white-spotted rose anemone, top, has its tentacles retracted. Anemones have stinging cells called nematocysts that help them stun and then capture shrimps and small fishes.

PACIFIC SPECIES
This anemone and California sea cucumber can be seen in the Pacific Northwest exhibits, which are adjacent to the Gulf of Maine exhibits.

GIANT PACIFIC OCTOPUS
Octopuses have the ability to change both their color and texture. These invertebrates are intelligent and very strong. Using their eight arms, they can move more than 700 pounds.

AMERICAN LOBSTER
American lobsters are a cultural icon and one of the most important fisheries in New England. But it takes seven years for these lobsters to reach one pound—the minimum legal harvest size.

BREAKTHROUGH

In 2007, under director of research Michael Tlusty, the New England Aquarium's American Lobster Research Program developed a model for studying lobster shell disease in a laboratory. A bacterial infection that eats away at lobsters' shells, the disease makes the animals unsuitable for market, damaging the lobster fishery. The laboratory model was made possible by $150,000 in funding from Rhode Island Sea Grant.

GULF OF MAINE

From rocky beaches to deep-water boulder reefs to sandy sea floors, the Gulf of Maine bursts with life. This habitat, which stretches from Cape Cod to Canada, is highlighted in six exhibits that cover more than half of the Aquarium's third level. Almost all of New England's marine environments are featured here, from the Eastport Harbor with its spiny sunstars, basket stars and redfish to the Isles of Shoals, which houses some of the Aquarium's most unusual animals: rare blue and white lobsters.

The centerpiece of the exhibit is a 2,500-gallon bow-front tank depicting a Stellwagen boulder reef community—a glacial deposit habitat on the ocean floor. This tank includes brightly colored anemones, sea stars, sun stars and rosefish. Nearby is a sandy bottom community that is home to Atlantic cod, halibut and chain dogfish sharks. These fish are joined by various species of skates, which scavenge for crustaceans, worms, fish and mollusks along the sea floor. Another distinctive bottom-dweller in the Gulf of Maine is the goosefish, a broad-mouthed, flattened fish with mottled brown coloring. Finally, piping plovers, sanderlings, terns and other New England birds populate the shorebirds exhibit, including several that have been rescued and rehabilitated from the local Cape shore.

SPINY SUNSTAR
Inside the Gulf of Maine's boulder reef exhibit, a spiny sunstar sits on the rocks next to a rose sea anemone and a whelk egg mass.

GOOSEFISH
Goosefish release long masses that float in the water. From these masses, eggs develop and little goosefish larvae are hatched. These egg veils can be 60 feet long, three feet wide and contain one to two million eggs. The Aquarium's goosefish usually lays a veil every year.

SEA ANEMONE
Sea anemones like this northern red anemone at top are a common sight on the rocky bottoms and tidepools of the New England sea.

SHOREBIRD SURVIVORS

In addition to rehabilitating turtles and other marine animals, the Aquarium has received several rescued shorebirds. One dunlin was found along the Cape Cod Canal in 2003 with a fractured left wing.

When she was done with her rehabilitation at the Cape Wildlife Center, she could fly a little but not well enough to make her annual breeding migration. (For shorebirds, this migration usually covers thousands of miles, from as far south as Texas all the way to northern Hudson Bay in Canada.) As a result, she found a permanent home at the Aquarium. Another bird in the shorebird exhibit, a piping plover, hatched on New Seabury Beach in June 2003. Shortly after, he was observed with an injured wing, so he was corralled and brought to a rehabilitation center on Cape Cod. There, veterinarians found two breaks in his left wing and determined that he would never fly again. He too is now a resident in the shorebird exhibit.

BLUE LOBSTER
The Aquarium often has rare blue lobsters like this one on exhibit. Lobsters are normally a blend of brown and green.

RELATIVELY FAST
This spiny sun star can move relatively quickly for a sea star, reaching speeds of up to 27 inches per minute! Spiny sun stars dislike exposure to air while the tide recedes; instead they stalk their prey most often in subtidal zones.

BENEATH THE HARBOR
This photograph shows a horse star on the window of the Eastport Harbor exhibit, which replicates a rocky habitat. Horse stars feed on other stars and worms. Behind it is a redfish, also known as a sea perch.

GROUP OF STARS
Unlike some species of sea stars, Northern sea stars are not cannibalistic, so they can congregate together like this. They eat by covering prey such as barnacles and mussels with their stomachs.

BREAKTHROUGH

Aquarium researchers conducted the first aerial surveys of bluefin tuna in the Gulf of Maine in 1995. To more accurately assess the numbers of bluefin tuna in the area, Aquarium researcher Molly Lutcavage gave tuna spotter pilots GPS data loggers and camera equipment. The findings led to major changes in the way the tuna are counted.

SUSTAINABLE SEAFOOD

Worldwide, many popular types of seafood are becoming less common due to overfishing and loss of habitat. In many cases, the industry relies on environmentally destructive fishing and farming techniques. However, there are things that supermarkets, restaurants and other seafood companies can do to ensure that their seafood is not caught or farmed using methods that damage surrounding ecosystems. The Aquarium is working with a number of companies and other conservation organizations to encourage the development of ocean-friendly aquaculture and wild-caught fishery operations.

To help engage consumers and chefs, the Aquarium has developed several sustainable seafood programs that promote ocean-friendly seafood. These programs encourage the responsible management of fishery resources; provide support to regional and international fishing communities, industries and organizations; educate consumers about which types of seafood are more environmentally friendly than others; and even provide delicious ocean-friendly seafood recipes.

POISON DART FROG
Poison dart frogs have toxic chemicals under their skin. Their gleaming colors warn predators to stay away.

AMAZON RAINFOREST

The Aquarium's seven Amazon exhibits include several windows that reach nearly to the floor, immersing visitors in a replica of South America's lush rivers and forests. The habitats feature hundreds of live plants and accurate recreations of enormous rainforest trees, vines and termite mounds, some flooded by river water. Piranhas, anacondas, electric eels and freshwater stingrays swim through the exhibits, while a Surinam toad, colorful poison dart frogs and jewel-like schools of cardinal tetra fishes hide among the rocks and plants.

The Amazon rainforest—one of the most diverse habitats in the world—undergoes a unique change every year. For several months, the river floods thousands of square miles of forest. Many fishes take advantage of this flood to eat the fruits, seeds and insects that are within reach when the forest is underwater. One particular fish, the pacu, can grow to more than two feet long just by eating its favorite food: the seeds that drop from forest trees. By filling up during the flood, this fish builds up fatty reserves that help it survive the challenges of the low-water season. Other seed-eaters of the Amazon include the silver dollar fish and the yellow-spotted side-necked turtle. They help distribute plant populations by eating the seeds and digesting them along the river.

DID YOU KNOW?

Researchers have discovered that when food is scarce, piranhas "bark," "croak" and make drum-like percussion sounds. These noises serve as a warning to intimidate competitors for food.

GETTING DEFENSIVE
Contrary to what many people believe, piranhas traveling in big groups are actually taking cover, not on the attack. Individual piranhas are more likely to survive a dolphin river attack when swimming in a group. This defensive behavior is called shoaling.

YELLOW-SPOTTED SIDE-NECKED TURTLE
As one of the freshwater turtle species at the Aquarium, the yellow-spotted side-necked turtle lives among the roots of the Amazon Rainforest exhibit.

RAISING THEM WELL
Many species of poison dart frogs raise their tadpoles safely above predators in tiny ponds that gather in the leaves of air plants, or bromeliads.

RED BELLIED PIRANHA
These fish eat small worms, insects or fishes—all items they can find throughout the Amazon River basin.

SEVERUM
Two severum swim among the tree trunks in the flooded forest exhibit of the Amazon Rainforest. Their rounded fins help them maneuver easily as they search for insects, fishes and plants to eat among the roots.

GREEN ANACONDA
The anaconda is one of the world's largest snakes, living in dark pools and rivers throughout Central and South America. This species can grow to be 30 feet long.

DID YOU KNOW?

Snakes don't have eyelids, and they never blink. Instead, a modified scale over their eyes protects their sensitive ocular tissue from damage. One of the first signs a snake is going to shed its skin is having cloudy eyes. The eyes turn milky in color while the new layer is formed.

SEA STAR
There are more than 2,000 species of sea stars. Since water is pumped directly into their bodies, sea stars have little or no ability to filter pollutants and toxins. This makes them highly susceptible to damage from pollution and contaminants.

EDGE OF THE SEA TOUCH TANK

At the Edge of the Sea Touch Tank and tide pool, visitors can touch a sea urchin, meet a lobster or hold a hermit crab in their hands. They might even spot hermit crab larvae sparkling on the surface of the water. Juvenile sea stars can also inhabit the exhibit, but visitors are unlikely to notice them. These miniscule creatures can only be seen with a microscope and are shaped much differently than the adults. Adult sea stars are the most recognizable inhabitants. Commonly known as starfish, these animals are not fish but invertebrates that circulate salt water throughout their body and use it to propel their tube feet. Other popular animals in the touch tank include horseshoe crabs and periwinkles (small marine snails).

At the touch tank, there is always an Aquarium educator present to answer any questions and advise guests on how to handle the animals properly. Animals should be picked up gently and supported fully in the palm of the hand—never pried or pulled from a rock or other surface. Visitors are encouraged to keep animals underwater as much as possible. It is much less stressful for the animals and is also the best way to observe their behavior.

DID YOU KNOW?

Horseshoe crabs are critical for medical research. Their blood has special properties, and they possess one of the most effective antibiotic systems in nature. The Food and Drug Administration (FDA) requires that their blood be used to test batches of injectable human and animal medication to ensure they are free of bacterial contamination.

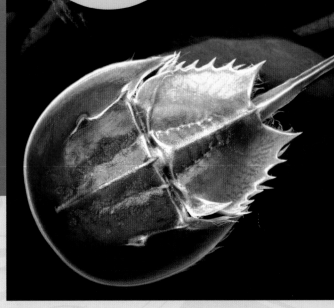

HORSESHOE CRAB
Horseshoe crabs are arthropods, meaning they are closely related to spiders and scorpions in addition to shrimps, crabs and lobsters.

EXPLORING THE TIDEPOOLS
Animal educators are always on hand to answer questions about the animals in Edge of the Sea Touch Tank. The New England Aquarium was the first public aquarium to have a touch tank.

HERMIT CRAB
Female long-clawed hermit crabs, such as this one at right, carry their eggs for several weeks before releasing the larvae into the water.

SEADRAGONS

There are only two species of seadragons in the world—leafy and weedy—and the New England Aquarium displays them both. Despite their fearsome name, seadragons—which are actually fish—don't have any teeth. Instead of biting, they suck food down their long tube snouts. Leafy seadragons can be 14 inches in length, while weedy seadragons are slightly larger, attaining 18 inches.

Seadragons can change color depending on age, diet and stress levels. Weedy seadragons are typically reddish-colored and lack the ornate, complex series of "branches" that characterize the leafy species. Both use their exceptional camouflage to hide from hungry predators on the temperate reefs of southern Australia. Unlike tropical coral reefs, temperate reefs are dominated by seaweed, algae, boulders and soft corals—the perfect environment for these solitary creatures to blend in. In the wild, they are often mistaken for floating pieces of algae. The Australian government protects seadragons through strict laws that prevent people from collecting or exporting the animals without permission. Even so, many scientists believe they are becoming less common, threatened by pollution and habitat destruction.

EAR RINGS
Seadragons have growth rings on their ear bones, which help scientists determine their age. Their lifespan ranges from 8 to 10 years.

WEEDY SEADRAGON
Weedy seadragons have less ornate branches, but can grow to be larger than leafy seadragons.

LEAFY SEADRAGON
Leafy seadragons, seen at top, are found only in South Australia. They are considered near threatened. Although the Australian government strictly forbids the capture of these animals, many of them are illegally harvested for use in alternative medicine.

MALE DELIVERY
Female seadragons lay up to 300 eggs, which the males carry around on a brood patch near the base of their tail. After six to eight weeks, the baby seadragons hatch and swim away. They are completely independent from the moment they hatch.

GLOBAL EXPLORERS

In 2009, senior aquarist Jeremy Brodt was awarded a grant to dive off the coast of South Australia to observe seadragons' mating habits and natural behaviors. Although these creatures are iconic and extraordinary, researchers have surprisingly limited knowledge about their life cycle and habits. This is largely a result of their cryptic nature. Brodt, however, was able to observe the animals and their habitat in detail. He uses this knowledge in managing the seadragon exhibit.

SEAHORSE HABITAT
The seahorse exhibit is located on the third level of the Aquarium. In the wild, seahorses live in diverse habitats, including shallow eelgrass, staghorn coral beds, shallow or calm harbors and under piers.

ON THEIR MENU
Seadragons eat small invertebrates—including shrimps and larval fishes—by sucking them through their long tube snouts.

GOOD NEIGHBORS
The seadragon exhibit includes 25 additional species of invertebrates and fishes that naturally coexist with seadragons.

SEAHORSES

Seahorses are more widespread than their seadragon cousins, with several dozen known species found in temperate or warm salt waters. Yet most of the species worldwide are under threat due to overexploitation, harvesting, pollution and habitat degradation. Like all fishes, seahorses have gills for breathing, fins for swimming and an internal skeleton. Because of their poor ability to swim, seahorses do not flee from their enemies. They simply change color, camouflaging themselves in their environment.

Seahorses are unique among fishes in that they mate for life. Like seadragons, the males are also responsible for childbearing. Male seahorses have a kangaroo-like brood pouch on their stomachs. During breeding season, their pouch receives eggs from the female. The male fertilizes the eggs in the pouch, where they will develop over the next 10 to 25 days. The young hatch in the pouch, and once they are ready, the male will release them to fend for themselves.

SCHOOLING FISHES

When staring at the shiny, moving wall of herring that inhabit the Aquarium's Schooling Exhibit, visitors find it can be difficult to focus on just one fish at a time. In fact, that's exactly the point. Groups of schooling fishes, like the blueback herring often found in this exhibit, can coordinate their movements to look like one big, shimmering blur. This makes it challenging for predators to pick out one particular fish and attempt to chase it down. Often all a predator can do is swim into a group with its mouth open and hope for the best—not the most effective or energy-efficient tactic. Moving in a big group also conserves energy for the fish by creating a series of small eddies that make it easier for them to swim.

The adaptations that make schooling behavior possible are almost like having a special sixth sense. These fish have an organ called a lateral line that runs down the length of their bodies. This ultra sensitive structure helps the fish detect the smallest change in movement or vibration in the water, allowing them to stay together when they travel.

SAFETY IN NUMBERS
Schooling behavior helps protect schooling fishes, like these bohar snappers, from predators like the reef sharks in the background of this photograph.

BOHAR SNAPPER
Bohar snappers are a schooling fish commonly found in coral reefs, sheltered lagoons and outer reefs around oceanic islands. Aquarium explorers have observed more snappers than expected in areas where shark populations have decreased.

BAHAMIAN GRUNT
Bahamian grunts are another species of schooling fish. They can be found in the Aquarium's Giant Ocean Tank.

GETTING SCHOOLED

The Schooling Fishes exhibit gives visitors a look at this fascinating behavior. In this photograph, blueback herring are schooling. The exhibit is populated with the help of the Massachusetts Division of Fisheries and Wildlife. Depending on the day, there can be more than 2,000 fish moving through the exhibit!

FLOWER HAT JELLY
These intricate animals are found off the coast of Southern Japan, Brazil and Argentina. They are thought to be quite rare, but their conservation status is not known.

DID YOU KNOW?

Jellies are hardy adaptors. Seasonal jellies seem to appear when the water is warm and seem to die when it gets cold, so climate change enables them to feed longer. In addition, they can exist in low-oxygen levels caused by pollution and advantageously feed on their stunned, oxygen-deprived prey.

SEA JELLIES

Mistakenly called jellyfish, sea jellies are not fish at all. Jellies have no backbone, no heart, and are 95 percent water. While they don't have a real brain, they do possess a sophisticated cluster of nerves. They are often found on the beach after a rough storm. Out of the water, jellies are shapeless, gelatinous blobs; yet underwater, they are beautiful, graceful swimmers.

Jellies have existed for hundreds of millions of years, lived in all the oceans of the world, inhabited some lakes and rivers—and have hardly changed. Their lack of a sophisticated body structure has allowed them to live simply. By just riding the ocean's currents, jellies can travel hundreds of miles. Most can move themselves toward the sunlight, a food source or the current by using their pulsing swimming style. Most jellies eat as they drift, catching plankton, fish eggs, larval fishes, invertebrates and small shrimp-like animals, while some actively hunt with their tentacles to capture a meal and then slowly pass the food toward their bell- or saucer-shaped body. If food is scarce, many jellies have the strategic ability to shrink in size, requiring less food. When food is abundant, they can expand. Out of approximately 2,000 jelly species, only about 70 are known to be harmful to humans.

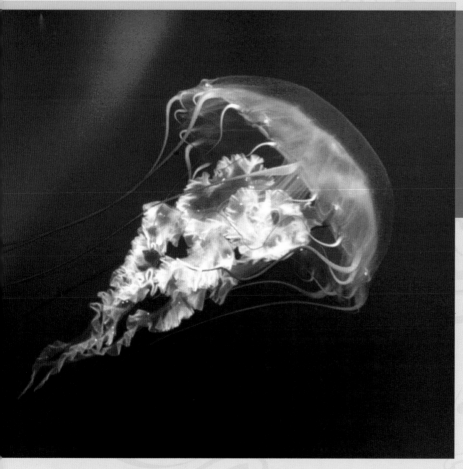

BLACK SEA NETTLE
Jellies are found in several areas around the Aquarium: on both floors of the West Wing, like this black sea nettle, and rotated into the Thinking Gallery on Level Two, like the flower hat jellies shown opposite.

SPOTTED AUSTRALIAN JELLY
Spotted Australian jellies, like this one at top, are one of the species found in the Aquarium's West Wing. While their native range is in Australia, these jellies have also been found along the southeastern coast of the United States.

POPULATION BOOM
Rising sea nettle populations have caused problems in many ocean areas, since those jellies consume fish eggs and larvae. Booming populations of sea nettles can affect regional fisheries as well because they often compete for the same food. The photograph above shows a Pacific sea nettle, cousin to some of the out-of-control sea nettle species.

NEW BALANCE FOUNDATION
MARINE MAMMAL CENTER

In the New Balance Foundation Marine Mammal Center, California sea lions dart through the water, and Northern fur seals show off their "flipper-stand"—the seal equivalent of a handstand. The Center's tank was designed to be a variety of depths in order to showcase different types of behaviors. The seals tend to groom and interact with visitors through the glass in the shallow area, while they use the deep end for diving and porpoising (where the animals generate enough speed to jump out of the water). The exhibit also has lifelike rocks that the seals and sea lions use for hauling out after a big swim, stretching and grooming. The fur seals in particular often rub against the rocks to scratch or groom their thick fur.

Each day, there are a series of training sessions that highlight the animals' flexibility and strength. Guests can watch the seals and sea lions race around, leap out of the water, spin, stretch and rest. In the summer, the seals and sea lions cool off with some of their favorite ice toys and by playing with the spray from a garden hose; in the winter, they love to frolic in the snow, which often blows into the open-air exhibit. Of course, all this activity requires a lot of fuel. Adult male fur seals and sea lions can consume as much as 30,000 calories per day, depending on the season. That means they can eat more than 500 fish per day. The females are considerably smaller than the males, requiring only about 5,000 calories per day. Nevertheless, that is twice the calories that the average person needs to maintain a healthy weight.

WAVE POOL
The Northern fur seals and California sea lions at the Marine Mammal Center participate in regular training sessions. Sometimes the frisky sea lions turn the tank into a wave pool!

CALIFORNIA SEA LION
California sea lions, top, are faster than any other seal or sea lion. They can swim at speeds up to 25 miles per hour.

SEALED WITH A KISS
The Aquarium's California sea lions and Northern fur seals are trained for enrichment and to build a trusting relationship that allows for regular medical checkups. This fur seal is practicing a kiss.

NORTHERN FUR SEAL
Fur seals and sea lions can spin while swimming underwater by maneuvering their front flippers in the same way that people use their arms to spin while skating.

GLOBAL EXPLORERS

In 2010, one of the Aquarium's marine mammal trainers, Patty Schilling, visited a remote Alaskan breeding island for Northern fur seals. Her purpose was to help conduct important population studies for this vulnerable species by counting pups. For three weeks, Schilling and other researchers from the National Oceanic and Atmospheric Administration (NOAA) sheared a small patch of fur from a predetermined number of pups. This harmless procedure helped researchers better estimate the number of fur seal pups born that year. (The patch filled in when the pups grew a new coat of fur.)

ON THE REBOUND
The Aquarium welcomed two California sea lion pups in 2011. California sea lions were hunted intensely in the 19th and early 20th centuries, and their populations declined. After laws were passed that protected marine mammals, their numbers rebounded in most places.

FUR FACTS
The Aquarium's trainers often share that Northern fur seals have the second thickest fur in the animal kingdom. (Sea otters have the thickest.)

ULTIMATE FRISBEE
Toys like this Frisbee are part of the sea lions' enrichment program. The sea lions also play with the hose in the exhibit, and sometimes trainers freeze bits of food in ice blocks for them.

HEALTHY, HAPPY, HAND-RAISED PUPS

The New Balance Foundation Marine Mammal Center is home to two rehabilitated sea lions. Found in Southern California, they were rejected by their mothers and hand-raised by staff and volunteers at the Santa Barbara Marine Mammal Center. California sea lions spend approximately one year with their mothers to learn how to forage, respond to predators and develop other skills necessary for survival. Since these two sea lions did not have any time with their mothers, the National Marine Fisheries Service (NMFS) determined that they were unlikely to survive in the ocean and began a search to find them a home in an aquarium or zoo.

The pups were flown to the New England Aquarium in the summer of 2011. One pup was eating fish on her own while the other was still transitioning from being fed formula to swallowing fish. Before the sea lion pups were introduced to the fur seals, they spent some time behind the scenes in quarantine to ensure they were healthy. This gave the staff time to develop a rapport with the pups, introduce them to the training program and establish some basic behaviors. The energetic pups quickly learned to follow the trainers around and started to get comfortable being touched along their sides. By the end of the summer, they were ready to participate in training sessions and joined the fur seals in the exhibit.

MARINE ANIMAL RESCUE

Established in 1968, the New England Aquarium's Marine Animal Rescue Team has responded to thousands of calls to rescue sea turtles, seals, porpoises, dolphins and whales. Its mission is to care for animals from Cape Cod through the New Hampshire coast that are stranded, injured or diseased. A marine animal is considered stranded when it is out of the ocean and unable to survive without assistance. Any whale, dolphin or porpoise on a beach is considered stranded. Seals, which are semi-aquatic, are only deemed stranded when they are sick or injured. Sea turtles are also semi-aquatic, but they only come up on land to nest. Since there are no nesting beaches in New England, a sea turtle on the beach in this part of the country needs immediate help.

Much of the Aquarium's marine rescue efforts are focused on these sea turtles. Each November, anywhere from 25 to 150 young sea turtles—most of them critically endangered Kemp's ridleys—are rescued from the chilly waters and beaches of Cape Cod Bay. Volunteer walkers from the Massachusetts Audubon Society comb miles of beach trying to find these sea turtles, which are then transported to the rescue team at the New England Aquarium.

Over the past 15 years, the Aquarium's Animal Care Center (sometimes called the "Sea Turtle Hospital") has treated and released hundreds of Kemp's ridley sea turtles as well as many green and loggerhead sea turtles. Most of them suffer from extreme hypothermia, severe dehydration, pneumonia and often shell or bone fractures. Around 86 percent survive after several months of treatment. The turtles capable of foraging for themselves are released back into the ocean. Each rehabilitated turtle brings conservationists a significant step closer to ensuring the survival of the species.

DID YOU KNOW?

Sometimes rescued turtles need to be placed on a diet so their weight gain isn't too excessive while in rehabilitation. This is necessary because, unlike their unlimited movements in the ocean, they are recovering in rehabilitation tanks. Special calculations are used to determine how many calories each turtle requires to maintain a healthy weight.

GOING HOME
When they are well enough, rehabilitated sea turtles are often released on the beach. Sometimes the release takes place on a boat.

KEMP'S RIDLEY
Adult Kemp's ridleys are preyed on by sharks and other large fishes. Humans also threaten them with fishing activities. The hatchlings are threatened by foxes, weasels, cats, dogs raccoons and crabs.

TURTLE RESCUE
Many rescued turtles are cold-stunned, which can happen in the fall when water temperatures drop. When turtles' temperatures fall below their tolerable limits, they lose the ability to hunt for food, eventually becoming susceptible to dehydration and disease.

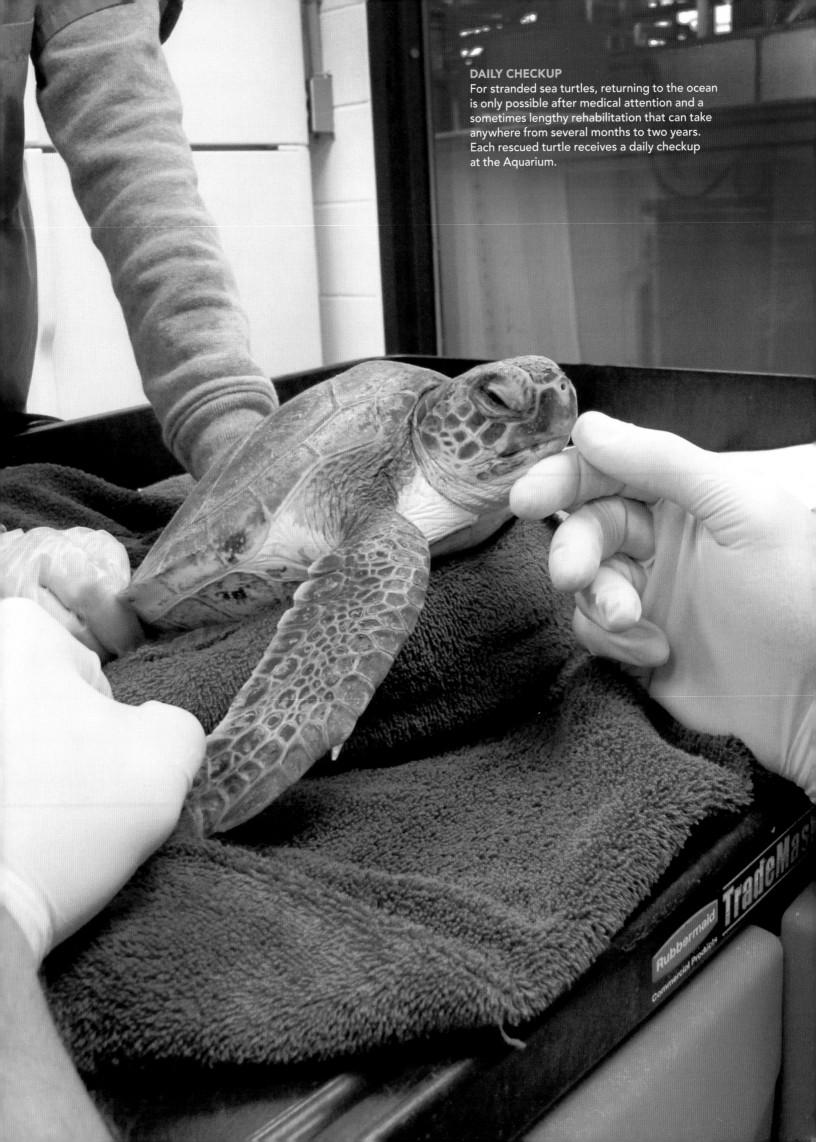

DAILY CHECKUP
For stranded sea turtles, returning to the ocean is only possible after medical attention and a sometimes lengthy rehabilitation that can take anywhere from several months to two years. Each rescued turtle receives a daily checkup at the Aquarium.

DID YOU KNOW?

The Aquarium encourages people to eat seafood—responsibly. In 2000, the Aquarium launched a Sustainable Seafood Program and began working with some of the world's largest seafood companies to encourage the sustainable development of farmed and wild-caught seafood resources. Today, the Aquarium also does consumer outreach while continuing to work with seafood companies, chefs, fishermen and fish farmers to make proactive changes in their practices to protect the blue planet.

SUSTAINABLE SEAFOOD
A fishing vessel passes a volcano off the Aleutian Islands in the Bering Sea. New England Aquarium conservation experts evaluate wild fisheries and aquaculture operations worldwide, making recommendations for improving fishing and fish-farming practices.

A LEADER IN CONSERVATION

Today, the New England Aquarium is a global leader in public education, ocean exploration and marine conservation. The Aquarium uses innovative on-site, on-water and outreach programming to instill in visitors a lifelong connection to the ocean—in effect, building the next generation of ocean stewards. Of its annual 1.3 million-plus visitors, nearly half are school-age children. Another 100,000 or more New England students are served by the Aquarium's outreach programs, and more are reached through its Teen Internship program, Harbor Discoveries Camps and other resources offered to educators by the Aquarium's Teacher Resource Center. By focusing on ocean conservation, the Aquarium is inspiring audiences of all ages to *live blue*™.

Outside Boston's Central Wharf, the New England Aquarium has become a leader in the rescue and rehabilitation of marine animals, including endangered sea turtles. Since 1980, Aquarium scientists have coordinated a multi-pronged effort to reduce human-caused deaths of critically endangered North Atlantic right whales. These efforts have included protecting right whale breeding grounds and migratory routes from Canada to Florida. Aquarium staff members have also led the successful effort to create the Phoenix Islands Protected Area in the equatorial Pacific Ocean, one of the world's largest marine protected areas. The Aquarium has changed the way seafood is caught, bought, sold and consumed through its Sustainable Seafood Programs, and Aquarium researchers have investigated potential causes for lobster shell disease, which affects one of New England's most valuable natural resources.

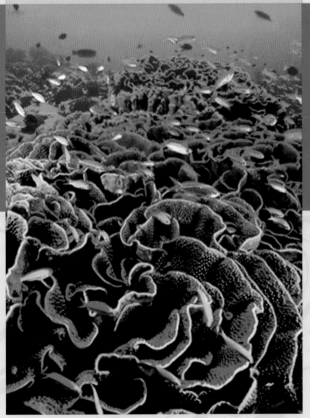

HEALTH ASSESSMENTS
It's impossible to collect blood from large whales through inches of blubber. However, Aquarium senior scientist Dr. Rosalind Rolland developed a new field of research that tests whale scat for hormone metabolites, red tide exposure, parasites and diet, providing information on whale reproduction, stress, disease and health.

PHOENIX ISLANDS PROTECTED AREA
The New England Aquarium, in partnership with the nation of Kiribati, led the charge to create the Phoenix Islands Protected Area. It was designated as a marine protected area in 2008.

NUDIBRANCH
Nudibranches are sea slugs, often with beautiful coloring. This one at top was photographed in Fiji during one of the Aquarium's collaborative expeditions.

FAMILY ALBUM
The Aquarium's right whale team maintains a photographic record of every known North Atlantic right whale, including this photograph depicting a mother and calf.

ON THE REEFTOP
A diver approaches a school of anthias on a reeftop during a dive at Namena Marine Reserve in Fiji. Aquarium explorers regularly return to these waters as part of a collaborative effort with other organizations.

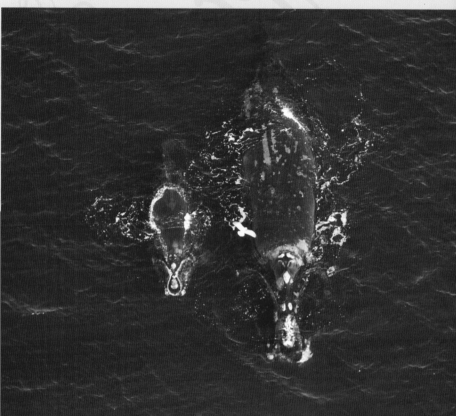

NORTH ATLANTIC RIGHT WHALE RESEARCH PROGRAM

Very little was known about North Atlantic right whales until an August 1980 survey, when New England Aquarium scientist Scott Kraus and a team of Aquarium researchers discovered 25 of them, including four calves in the Bay of Fundy between New Brunswick and Nova Scotia. These sightings provided the spark for more than three decades of Aquarium research on right whales that has led to groundbreaking conservation measures in the U.S. and Canada.

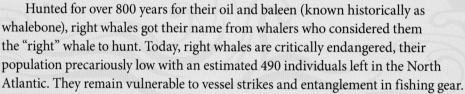

Hunted for over 800 years for their oil and baleen (known historically as whalebone), right whales got their name from whalers who considered them the "right" whale to hunt. Today, right whales are critically endangered, their population precariously low with an estimated 490 individuals left in the North Atlantic. They remain vulnerable to vessel strikes and entanglement in fishing gear.

The Aquarium's Right Whale Research Program is committed to protecting the remaining population and is the longest-running program of its kind in the world. Aquarium scientists have developed unique collaborations with the shipping and fishing industries to protect right whales throughout their range. For example, in 2003, Aquarium senior scientist Moira Brown—in cooperation with the Canadian government, Irving Oil Corporation, Canadian scientists at Dalhousie University, fishermen and other Canadian conservation organizations—spearheaded an effort to shift the commercial shipping lanes that run through the Bay of Fundy by approximately four nautical miles. This change reduced the probability of whale–ship collisions by 90 percent and led the way for similar protection from vessel strikes in all of the species' known habitats in the U.S. and Canada.

SCENT OF A WHALE
Fargo, a Rottweiler trained in scent detection, helps to locate right whale scat samples that will be analyzed for hormones, biotoxins and diseases.

GLOBAL EXPLORERS

Each August and September, Aquarium researchers head to Lubec, Maine, to observe the annual gathering of North Atlantic right whales in the Bay of Fundy. To monitor this species' status, the team maintains a photographic record of every known right whale and takes pictures of calves born over the winter. Aquarium vice president and scientist Scott Kraus developed the photo identification technique for the North Atlantic right whale. He and his colleagues Philip Hamilton, Amy Knowlton and Marilyn Marx have been to the bay so many times that they know the names and ID numbers of many of the whales on sight!

BARTLETT'S ANTHIAS
These Bartlett's anthias were photographed during an expedition to the Phoenix Islands in the equatorial Pacific Ocean.

HOW YOU CAN HELP

Thank you for visiting the New England Aquarium and purchasing this book as a way of taking the Aquarium experience home with you. The images and stories in these pages bring to life our 40-year tradition of protecting marine animals and promoting the importance of ocean conservation.

The oceans are such a powerful inspiration and such an essential resource that our visitors' early interactions with them can powerfully affect the rest of their lives. One of the amazing things about an institution like the Aquarium is the impact it has had on generations of visitors. Today, there are many leaders, researchers and authors in the field of ocean conservation who started out as wide-eyed young visitors here on Central Wharf.

The memories you take home from your visit and the stories you read here in this book are an invitation to join our long history of protecting the blue planet and to *live blue*™. Often the challenges facing our oceans seem insurmountable, but if we act together and make simple decisions to do what's right for the oceans, we can make a real difference.

Bud Ris
President and CEO

SCIENTIFIC EXPEDITIONS
Coral scientist Dr. David Obura gathers data during an expedition to the Phoenix Islands. The Aquarium periodically leads expeditions to the area to measure ecosystem health and work with partners in Kiribati.

live blue™

What does it mean to *live blue*™? It means making daily changes, big and small, that conserve resources and protect the environment. When we all make these small decisions together, they have a big impact.

- Choose ocean-friendly seafood.
- Buy local and organic produce, coffee and other household products, or try growing some of your own produce.
- Drive a fuel-efficient, low-polluting car.
- Choose to walk, bike or take public transportation whenever practical.
- Install energy-saving thermostats in your home.
- Install energy-efficient light bulbs and appliances.
- Eliminate lawn pesticides and choose native plants for your garden.
- Stay well informed and vote with the environment in mind.
- Use your consumer power—learn about the environmental practices of companies you buy from.
- Inspire your friends and family to also take action.

REMOTE ROCKHOPPERS
Rockhopper penguins, top, are threatened by pollution, climate change, overfishing and shifts in fish populations that have depleted their food sources. They breed in such remote and harsh locations that most have never encountered humans.

New England Aquarium

Protecting the blue planet

The New England Aquarium is one of the premier visitor attractions in Boston, with over 1.3 million visitors a year, and a major public education resource. The Aquarium is accredited by the Association of Zoos and Aquariums.

Special thanks to the following New England Aquarium staff members for their contributions to this book:

Bud Ris, *President and CEO*
Brian Skerry, *Explorer in Residence*
Scott Kraus, *Vice President of Research*
Jane Wolfson, *Vice President of Marketing and Communication*
Heather Tausig, *Associate Vice President of Conservation*
Steve Bailey, *Curator of Fishes*
Charles Innis, *VMD Director of Animal Health*
Kathy Streeter, *Curator of Marine Mammals*
Jenny Montague, *Assistant Curator of Marine Mammals*
Tony LaCasse, *Director of Media Relations*
Michael Tlusty, *Director of Research*
Anita Metzler, *Assistant Scientist and Laboratory Operations Manager*
Megan Riley, *Creative Director*
Jeff Ives, *Editorial Director*
Heather Urquhart, *Penguin Exhibit Manager*
Connie Merigo, *Rescue Department Manager/ Senior Biologist*
Moira Brown, *Senior Scientist*
John Mandelman, *Research Scientist*
Randi Rotjan, *Associate Scientist*
Bill Murphy, *Senior Aquarist*

New England Aquarium
Central Wharf • Boston, MA 02110
www.neaq.org
617-973-5200

Photo Credits
Unless otherwise indicated, all photos are copyright of the New England Aquarium.
William Bennett: *13b;* Alex Breisfoard: *51c;* Sam Cheng: *1a, 1c, 2a, 8b, 8c, 10a, 10b, 10c, 11a, 11b, 11c, 12, 13a, 14a, 14c, 15, 17a, 18a, 18c, 19, 20, 21a, 22a, 22b, 22c, 23, 24a, 25a, 25b, 26a, 26b, 26c, 27, 28, 29b, 29c, 30b, 31b, 31c, 33, 35c, 36a, 37a, 38, 41, 43a, 43c, 45a, 51b, 55a;* Randy Brogan: *14b, 17b; Cape Cod Times: 56c;* Jason Clermont: *58;* Kindra Clineff: *36c;* Dianne DeLucia: *44c;* Katherine Dooher: *7a, 53b;* Keith Ellenbogen: *16a, 48a, 48b, 52a, 54, 55b, 59b, 60a;* Cathy LeBlanc: *57;* Paul Erickson: *48c;* Jeff Fillman: *25c, 32a, 34, 35a, 35b, 36b, 39a, 44b, 47a, 47c, 50;* Nathan Fried Lipski: *52b, 52c, 53a;* Cat Holloway: *25d, 62, 63a;* Peter Nadeau: *40b;* Paul Nicklen: *59a;* EJ Ree: *32c;* Emmanuel Reyes: *32b, 40c;* Tony Rinaldo: *4b;* Lindsay Schiavoni: *30a;* Brian Skerry: *16b;* Jim Stringer: *24b;* Heather Urquhart: *13c;* Sarah Winchester: *17c*

New England Aquarium was developed by Beckon Books in cooperation with the New England Aquarium and Event Network. Beckon develops and publishes custom books for leading cultural attractions, corporations, and non-profit organizations. Beckon Books is an imprint of Southwestern Publishing Group, Inc., 2451 Atrium Way, Nashville, TN 37214. Southwestern Publishing Group, Inc., is a wholly owned subsidiary of Southwestern, Inc., Nashville, Tennessee.

Christopher G. Capen, *President, Beckon Books*
Monika Stout, *Design/Production*
Betsy Holt, *Writer/Editor*
www.beckonbooks.com
877-311-0155

Event Network is the retail partner of the New England Aquarium and is proud to benefit and support the Aquarium's mission of conservation, education, science, and recreation.
www.eventnetwork.com

ISBN: 978-1-935442-14-1
Printed in the United States of America
10 9 8 7 6 5 4 3 2 1